Cover Photo: David Wolff - Patrick / Contributor / Getty Images

ISBN 978-1-4950-2216-6

7777 W. BLUEMOUND RD. P.O. BOX 13819 MILWAUKEE, WI 53213

Visit Hal Leonard Online at
www.halleonard.com

STRUM AND PICK PATTERNS

This chart contains the suggested strum and pick patterns that are referred to by number at the beginning
of each song in this book. The symbols ⊓ and ∨ in the strum patterns refer to down and up strokes, respectively.
The letters in the pick patterns indicate which right-hand fingers play which strings.

p = thumb
i = index finger
m = middle finger
a = ring finger

For example; Pick Pattern 2
is played: thumb - index - middle - ring

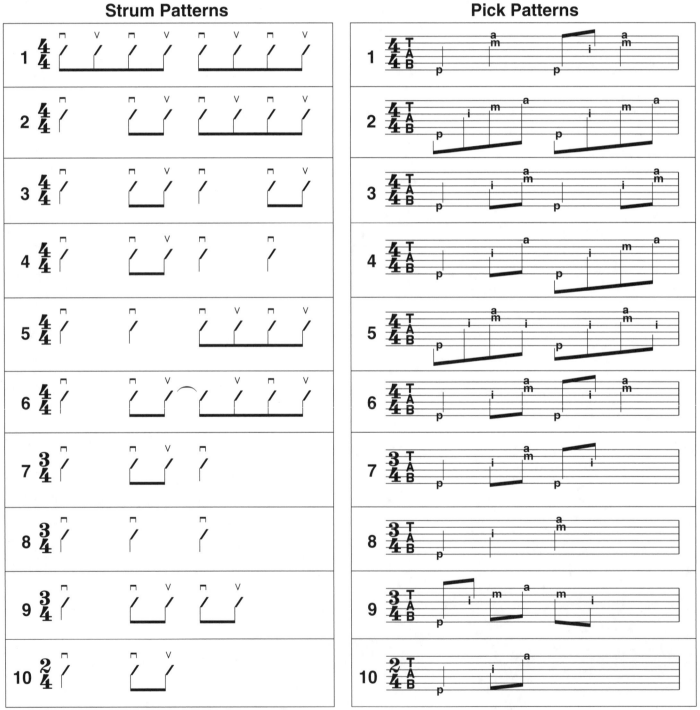

You can use the 3/4 Strum and Pick Patterns in songs written in compound meter (6/8, 9/8, 12/8, etc.).
For example, you can accompany a song in 6/8 by playing the 3/4 pattern twice in each measure.
The 4/4 Strum and Pick Patterns can be used for songs written in cut time (¢) by doubling the note
time values in the patterns. Each pattern would therefore last two measures in cut time.

Animals

Words and Music by Adam Levine, Ben Levin and Shellback

Strum Pattern: 6
Pick Pattern: 5

Chorus
Moderately slow

Ba - by, I'm prey - ing on you to - night, _ hunt you down, eat you a - live, _ just like

*Sung one octave higher.

an - i - mals, _ an - i - mals, _ like an - i - mals, _ -mals. _ May - be you think that you can hide. _ I can

**Sung one octave higher.

smell your scent for miles, _ just like an - i - mals, _ an - i - mals, _ like an - i - mals, _ -mals. _ Ba - by, I'm...

Verse

1. So what you're try'n' to do to me, it's like we can't stop, we're en - e - mies;
2. So if I run, it's not e - nough. You're still in my head, for - ev - er stuck,

*Sung one octave higher.

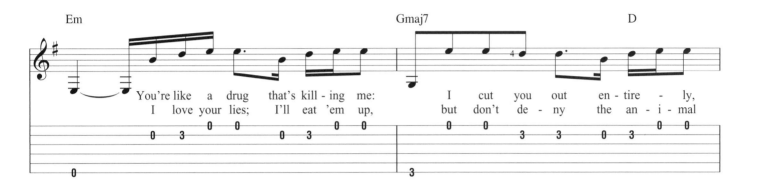

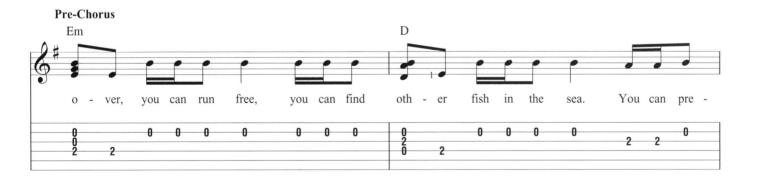

**Sung one octave higher.

Pre-Chorus

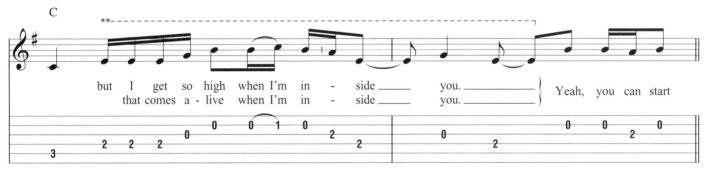

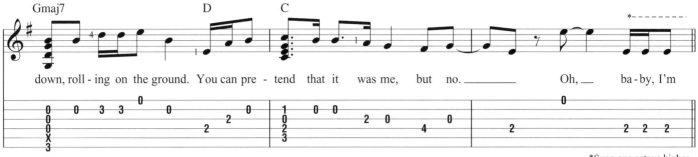

down, roll-ing on the ground. You can pre-tend that it was me, but no. _____ Oh, _ ba-by, I'm

*Sung one octave higher.

§ **Chorus**

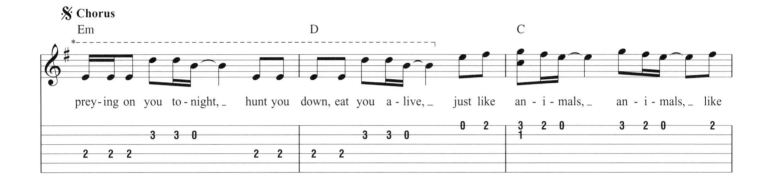

prey-ing on you to-night, _ hunt you down, eat you a-live, _ just like an-i-mals, _ an-i-mals, _ like

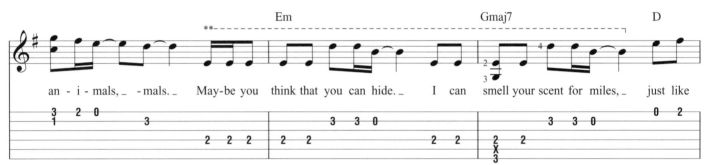

an-i-mals, _ -mals. _ May-be you think that you can hide. _ I can smell your scent for miles, _ just like

**Sung one octave higher.

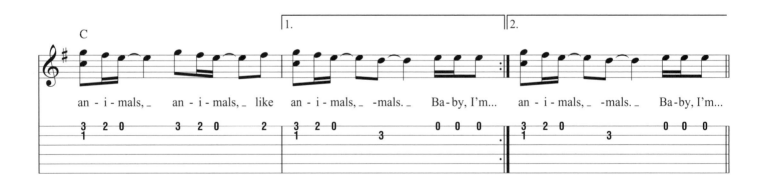

| 1. | | 2. |

an-i-mals, _ an-i-mals, _ like an-i-mals, _ -mals. _ Ba-by, I'm... an-i-mals, _ -mals. _ Ba-by, I'm...

Bridge

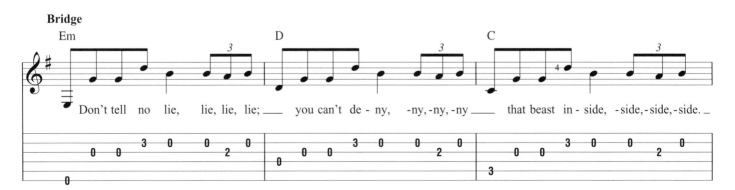

Don't tell no lie, lie, lie, lie; _ you can't de-ny, -ny,-ny,-ny _ that beast in-side, -side,-side,-side. _

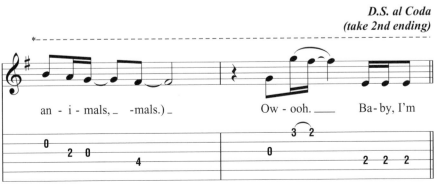

Daylight

Words and Music by Adam Levine, Max Martin, Sam Martin and Mason Levy

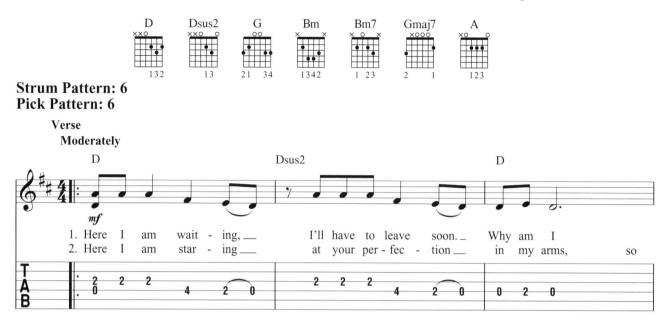

Strum Pattern: 6
Pick Pattern: 6

Verse
Moderately

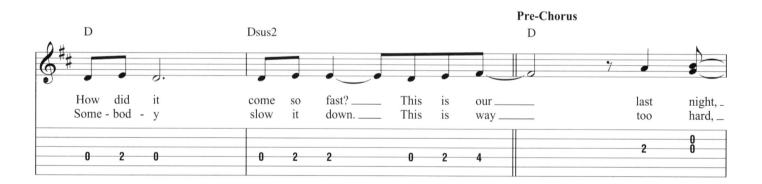

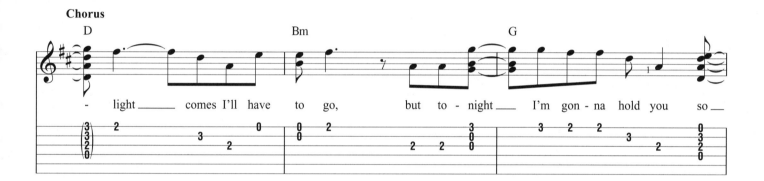

Chorus

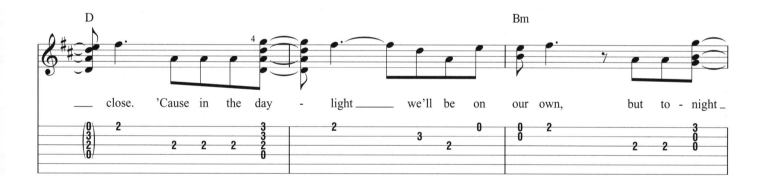

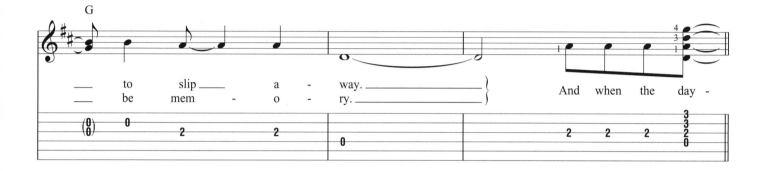

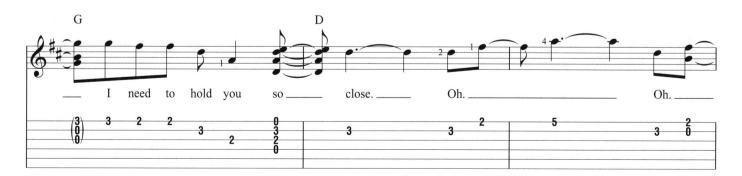

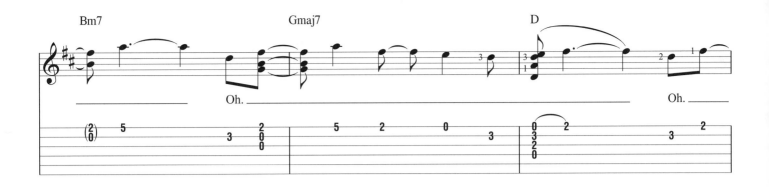

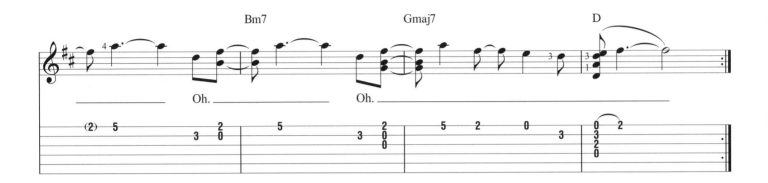

Bridge

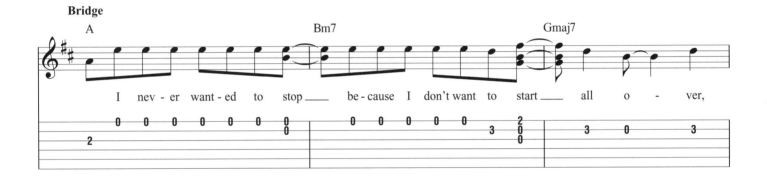

I nev-er want-ed to stop ___ be-cause I don't want to start ___ all o - ver,

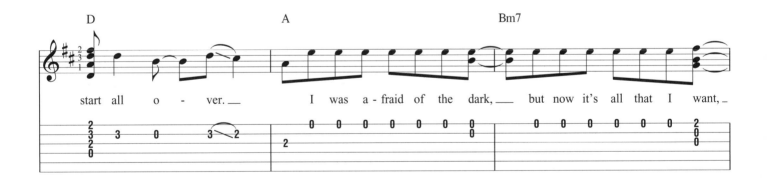

start all o - ver. ___ I was a-fraid of the dark, ___ but now it's all that I want, ___

___ all that ___ I want, all that ___ I want. And when the day-

*Let chord ring.

Chorus

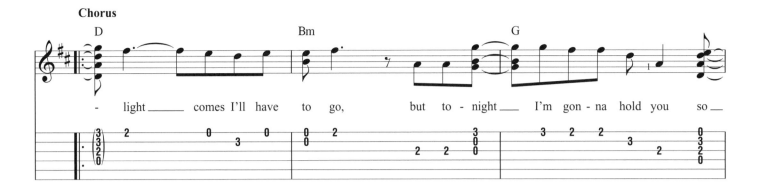

-light _____ comes I'll have to go, but to-night _____ I'm gon-na hold you so _____

_____ close. 'Cause in the day - light _____ we'll be on our own, but to-night _____

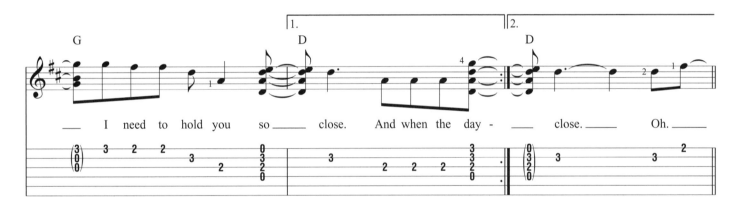

_____ I need to hold you so _____ close. And when the day- _____ close. _____ Oh. _____

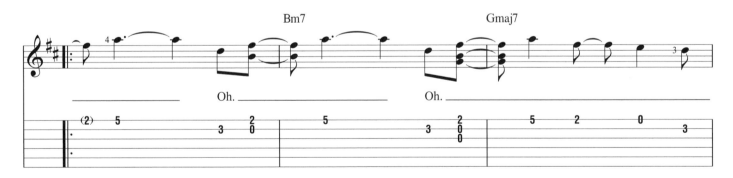

Oh. Oh.

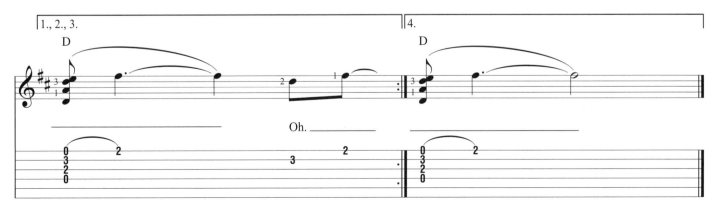

Oh.

Love Somebody

Words and Music by Adam Levine, Nathaniel Motte, Ryan Tedder and Noel Zancanella

*Capo I

Strum Pattern: 5
Pick Pattern: 1

*Optional: To match recording, place capo at 1st fret.

**Chord symbols reflect overall harmony.

1. I know your in - sides are feel - ing so hol - low,
2. You're such a hard act for me to fol - low,

oh, ___ oh, ___ oh, ___ and it's a hard pill for you to swal -
oh, ___ oh, ___ oh. ___ Love me to - day, don't leave me to - mor -

low, yeah. row, yeah. But if I

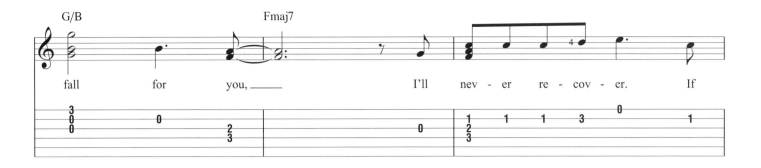

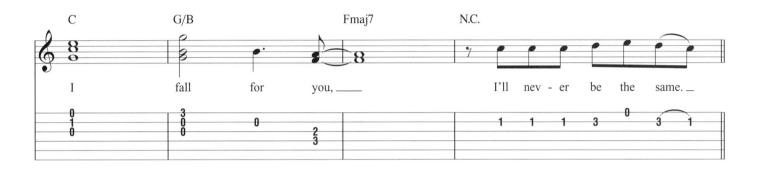

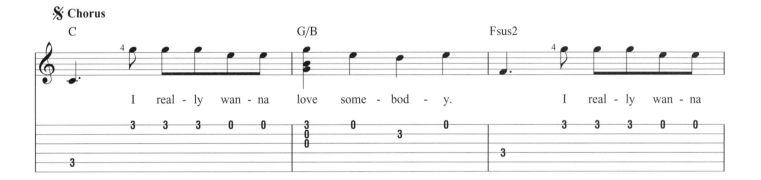

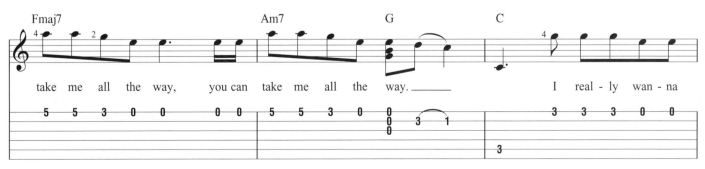

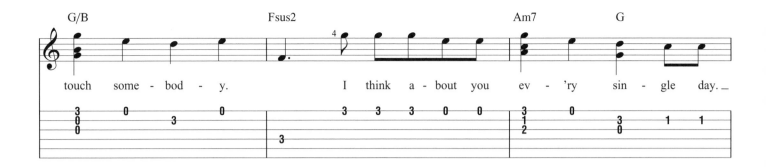

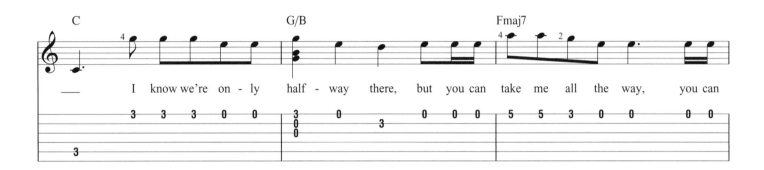

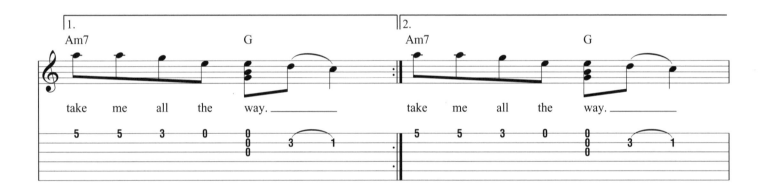

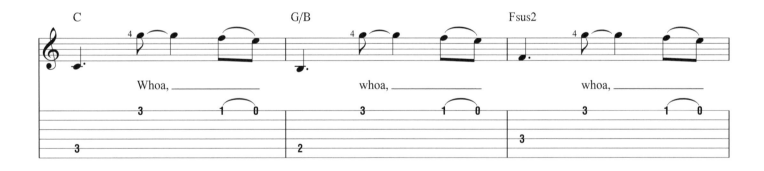

To Coda ⊕

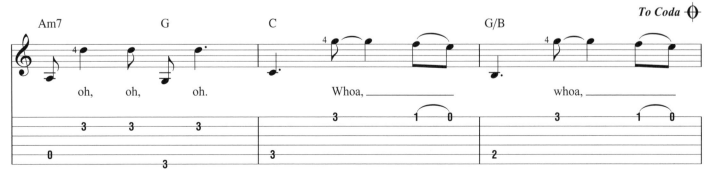

D.S. al Coda
(take 2nd ending)

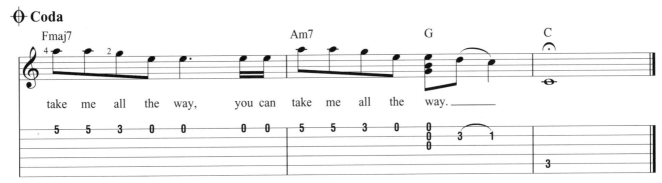

Makes Me Wonder

Words by Adam Levine
Music by Adam Levine, Jesse Carmichael and Mickey Madden

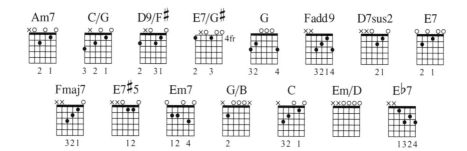

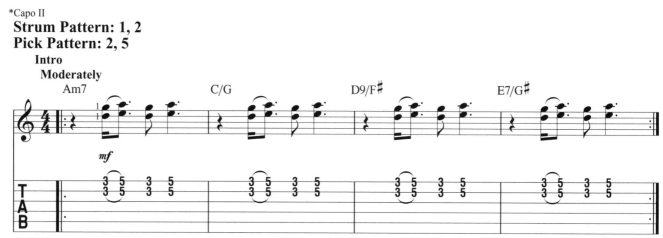

*Capo II

Strum Pattern: 1, 2
Pick Pattern: 2, 5

Intro
Moderately

*Optional: To match recording, place capo at 2nd fret.

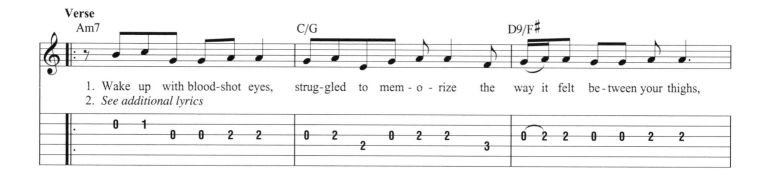

1. Wake up with blood-shot eyes, strug-gled to mem-o-rize the way it felt be-tween your thighs,
2. *See additional lyrics*

pleas-ure that made you cry. Uh, feels so good to be bad, not worth the af-ter-math. Af-

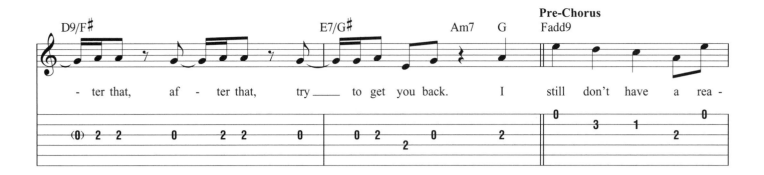

-ter that, af - ter that, try ___ to get you back. I still don't have a rea-

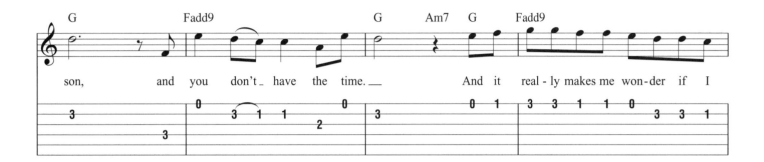

son, and you don't _ have the time. ___ And it real - ly makes me won-der if I

𝄋 Chorus

ev - er gave a fuck a - bout you. Give me some-thin' to be - lieve in 'cause I

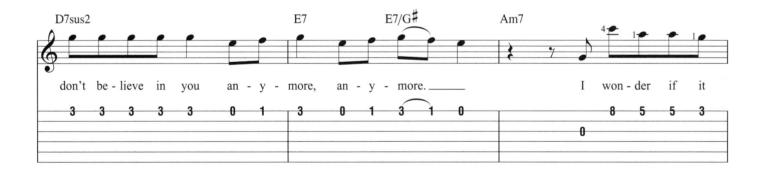

don't be - lieve in you an - y - more, an - y - more. ___ I won - der if it

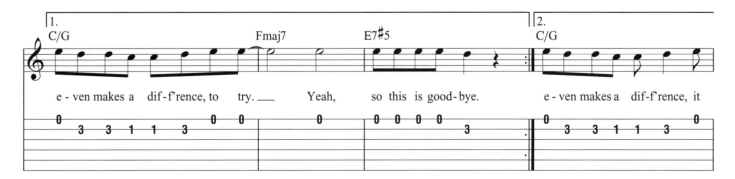

e - ven makes a dif - f'rence, to try. ___ Yeah, so this is good-bye. e - ven makes a dif - f'rence, it

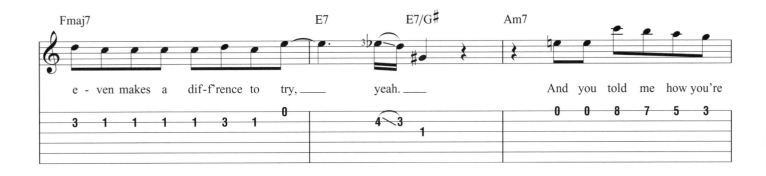

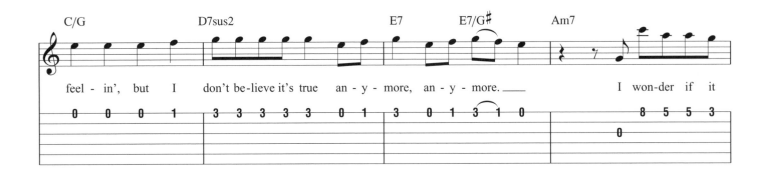

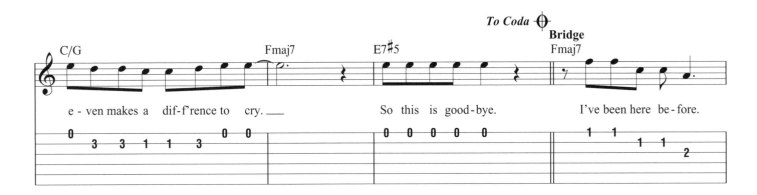

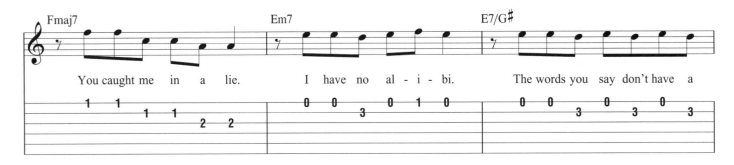

Pre-Chorus

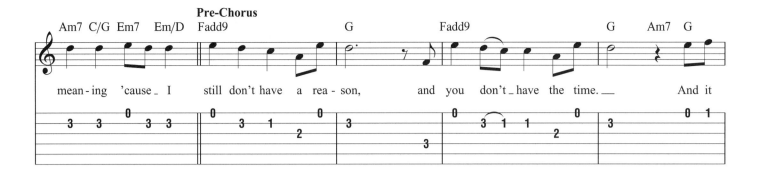

mean-ing 'cause_ I still don't have a rea-son, and you don't_ have the time.___ And it

real-ly makes me won-der if I ev-er gave a fuck a-bout you and I, and

D.S. al Coda
(take 2nd ending)

so this is good-bye. ___

Coda

Outro

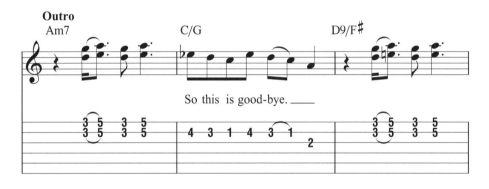

So this is good-bye. ___

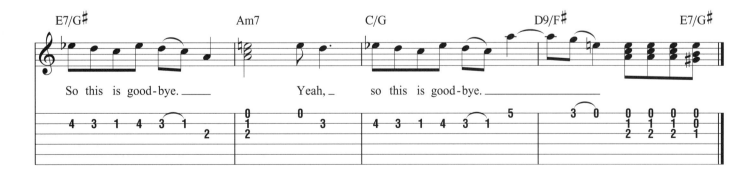

So this is good-bye. ___ Yeah, _ so this is good-bye. _____

Additional Lyrics

2. Goddamn, my spinnin' head, decisions that make my bed.
Now I must lay in it and deal with things I've left unsaid.
I want to dive into you, forget what you're goin' through.
I get behind; make your move. Forget about the truth.

Moves Like Jagger

Words and Music by Adam Levine, Benjamin Levin, Ammar Malik and Johan Schuster

*Optional: To match recording, place capo at 2nd fret.

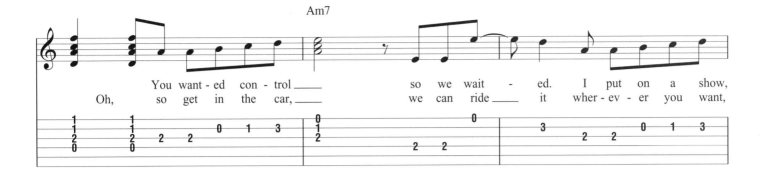

𝄋 Chorus

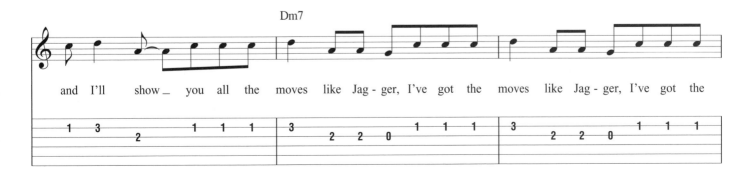

moves _____ like Jag - ger.   I don't need to try

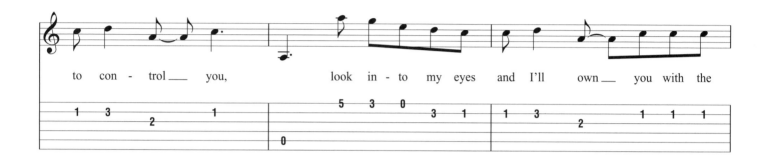

to con - trol ___ you,   look in - to my eyes and I'll own ___ you with the

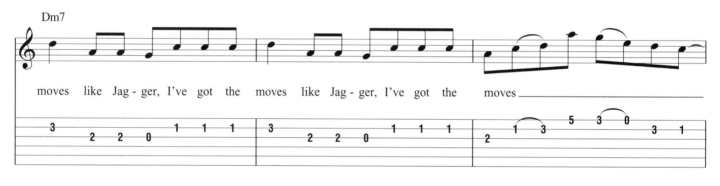

moves like Jag - ger, I've got the moves like Jag - ger, I've got the moves _____

1.   **2.**   *To Coda* ⊕ **Bridge**

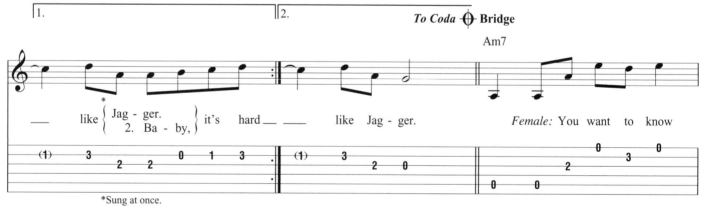

___ like { Jag - ger. / 2. Ba - by, } it's hard ___ ___ like Jag - ger.   *Female:* You want to know

*Sung at once.

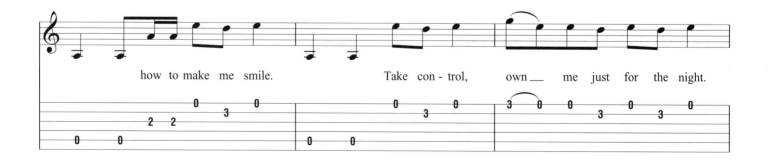

how to make me smile.   Take con - trol, own ___ me just for the night.

D.S. al Coda
(take 2nd ending)

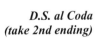

✛ **Coda**
Outro

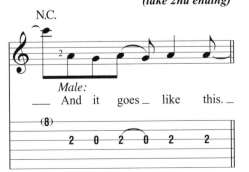

One More Night

Words and Music by Adam Levine, Johan Schuster and Max Martin

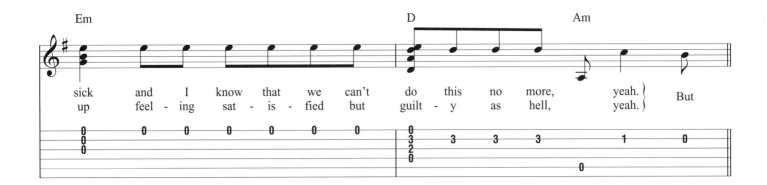

sick and I know that we can't do this no more, yeah. But
up feel - ing sat - is - fied but guilt - y as hell, yeah.

Pre-Chorus

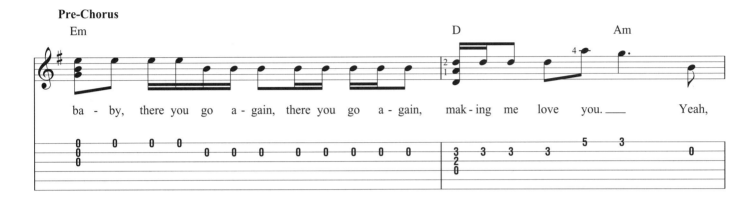

ba - by, there you go a - gain, there you go a - gain, mak - ing me love you. ___ Yeah,

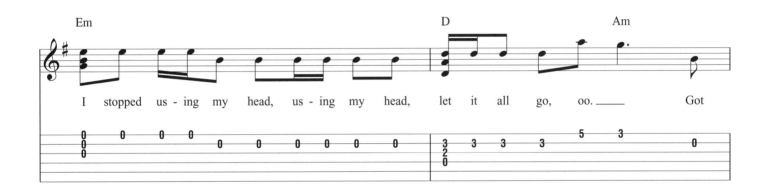

I stopped us - ing my head, us - ing my head, let it all go, oo. ___ Got

you stuck on my bod - y, on my bod - y like a tat - too. ___ And

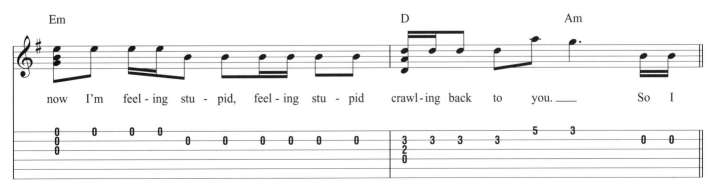

now I'm feel - ing stu - pid, feel - ing stu - pid crawl - ing back to you. ___ So I

Chorus

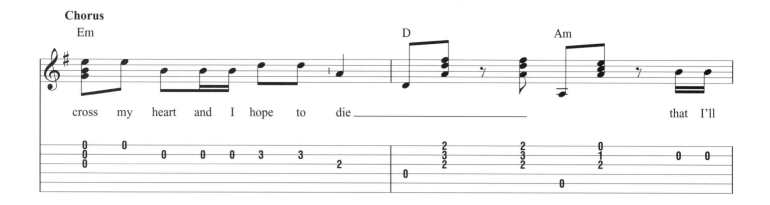

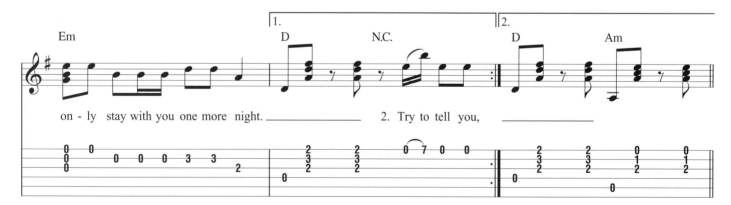

Bridge

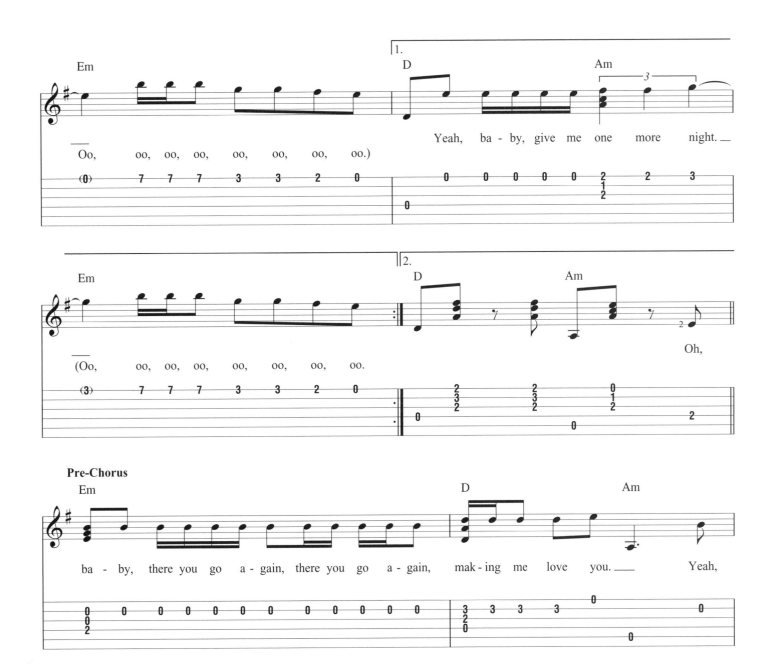

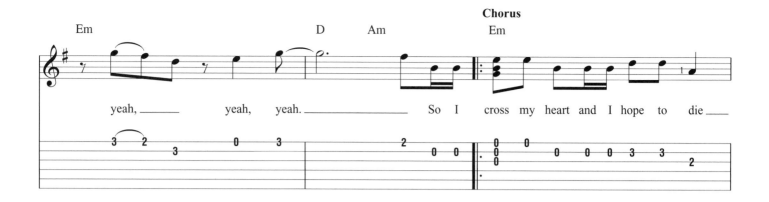

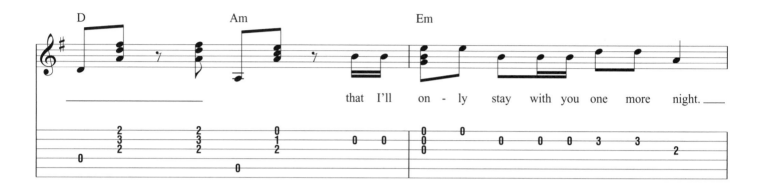

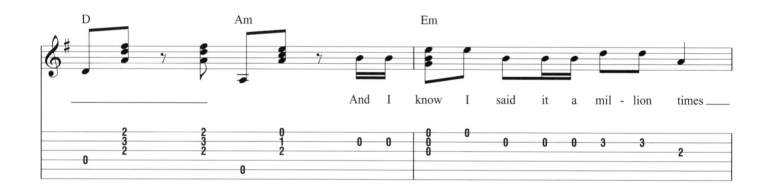

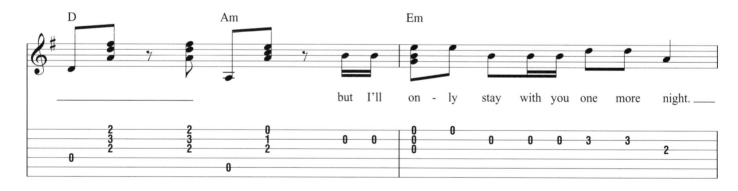

She Will Be Loved

Words and Music by Adam Levine and James Valentine

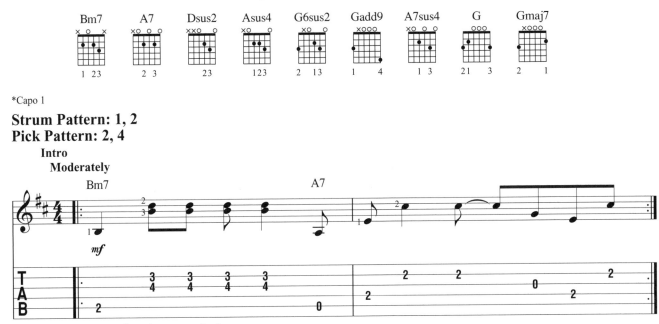

*Capo 1

Strum Pattern: 1, 2
Pick Pattern: 2, 4

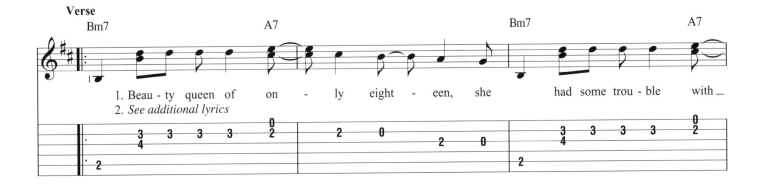

*Optional: To match recording, place capo at 1st fret.

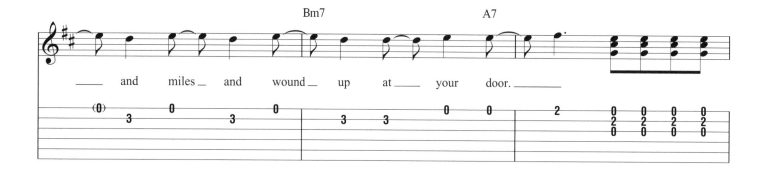

___ and miles ___ and wound ___ up at ___ your door. _____

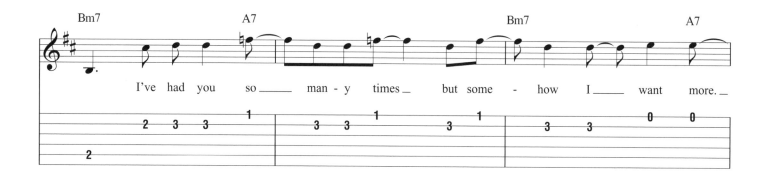

I've had you so ___ man - y times ___ but some - how I ___ want more. __

%. Chorus

_____ I don't mind spend - ing ev - er - y day ___

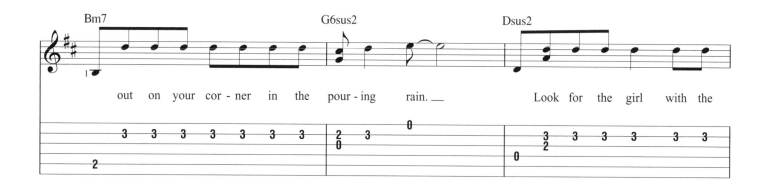

out on your cor - ner in the pour - ing rain. ___ Look for the girl with the

To Coda ⊕

bro - ken smile, ___ ask her if she wants to stay a - while. ___ And she will ___

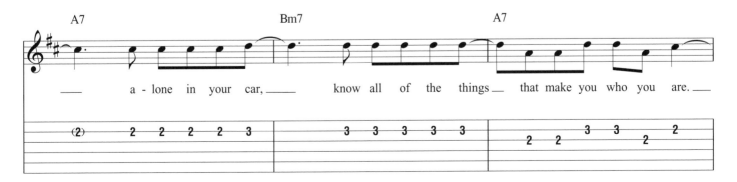

D.S. al Coda

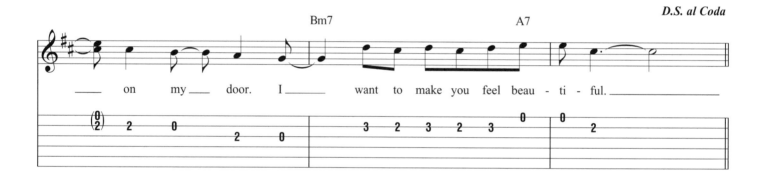

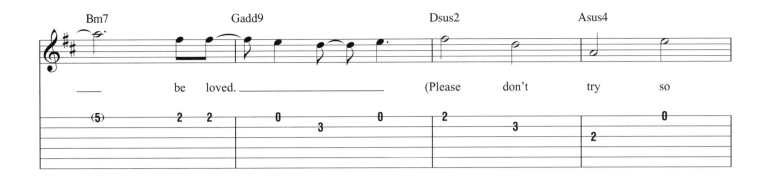

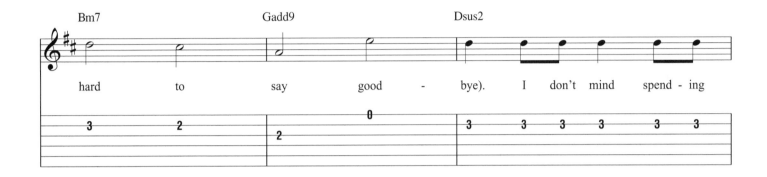

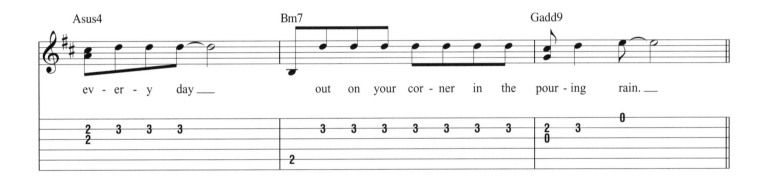

Outro

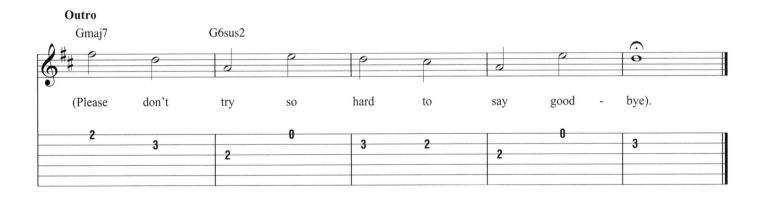

Additional Lyrics

2. Tap on my window, knock on my door.
   I want to make you feel beautiful.
   I know I tend to get so insecure,
   Doesn't matter anymore.
   It's not always rainbows and butterflies,
   It's compromise that moves us along, yeah.
   My heart is full and my door's always open,
   You come anytime you want, yeah.

Sugar

**Words and Music by Adam Levine, Henry Walter, Joshua Coleman,
Lukasz Gottwald, Jacob Kasher Hindlin and Mike Posner**

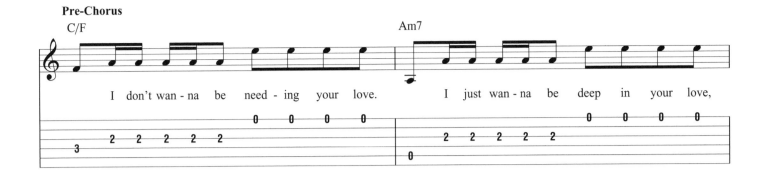

I don't wan - na be need - ing your love. I just wan - na be deep in your love,

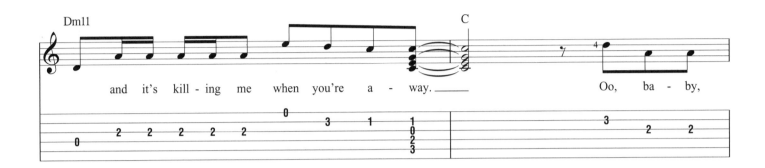

and it's kill - ing me when you're a - way. _____ Oo, ba - by,

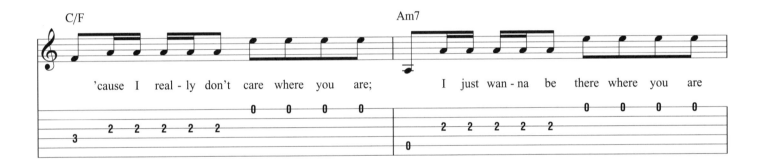

'cause I real - ly don't care where you are; I just wan - na be there where you are

and I got - ta get one lit - tle taste. _____ You're sug -

*Sung one octave higher, next 7.5 meas.

%Chorus

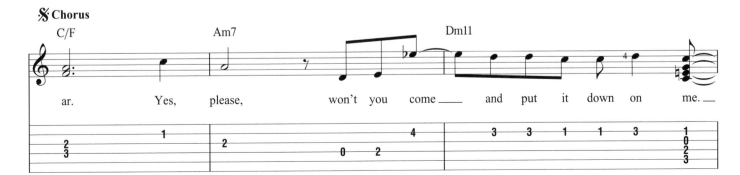

ar. Yes, please, won't you come _____ and put it down on me. _____

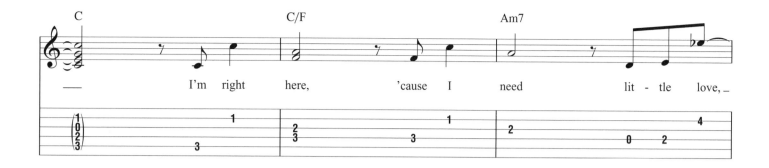

I'm right here, 'cause I need lit-tle love, ____

____ a lit-tle sym-pa-thy. ____ Yeah, you show ____ me good lov-ing, make ____

*Sung as written.

____ it al-right. Need ____ a lit-tle sweet-ness in my life. _____ You're sug -

**Sung one octave higher., next 4 meas.

3rd time, To Coda 1

4th time, To Coda 2

ar. Yes please, won't you come ____ and put it down on me. ____

Bridge

I want that red vel-vet; I want that sug-ar sweet. Don't let no-bod-y touch it

***Sung as written.

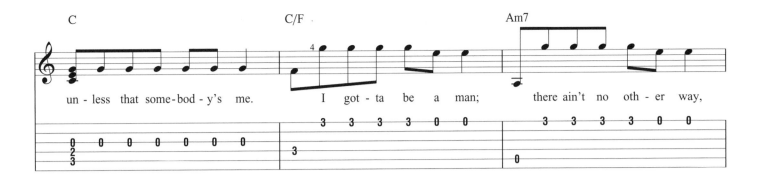

un - less that some-bod - y's me. I got-ta be a man; there ain't no oth-er way,

'cause girl, you're hot - ter than a south-ern Cal - i - for-nia day. I don't wan-na play no games;

D.S. al Coda 1

I don't got-ta be a-fraid. Don't give me all that shy shit, no make-up on. That's my sug -

Sung one octave higher.

⊕ Coda 1   *D.S. al Coda 2*   **⊕ Coda 2**   **Outro**

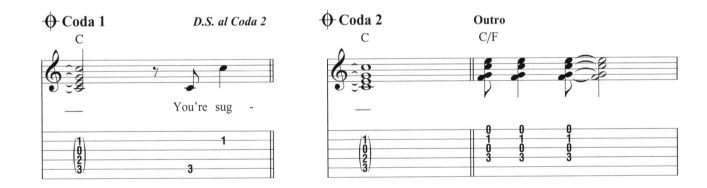

You're sug -

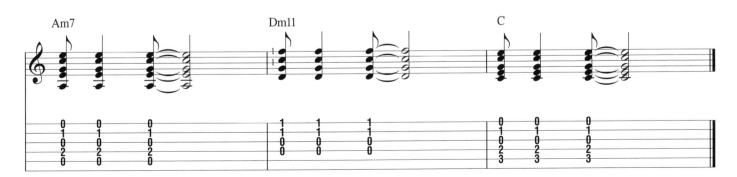

Sunday Morning

Words and Music by Adam Levine and Jesse Carmichael

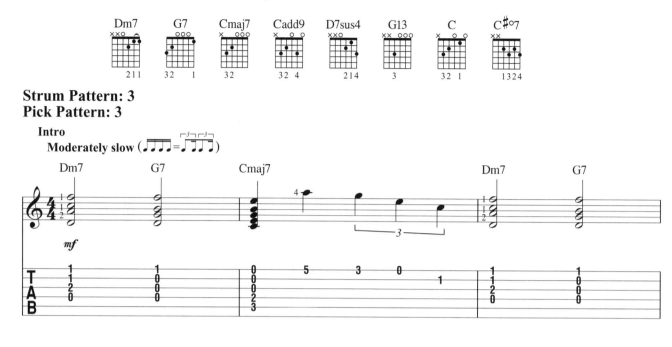

Strum Pattern: 3
Pick Pattern: 3

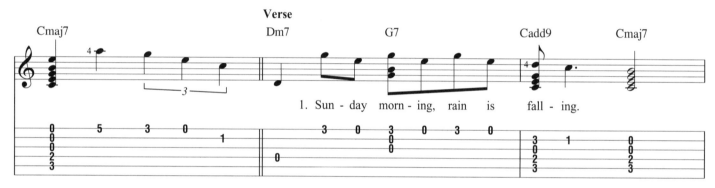

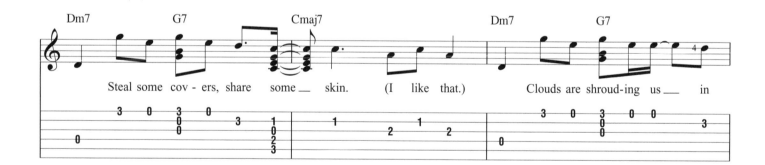

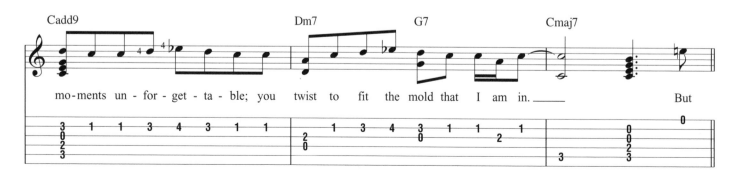

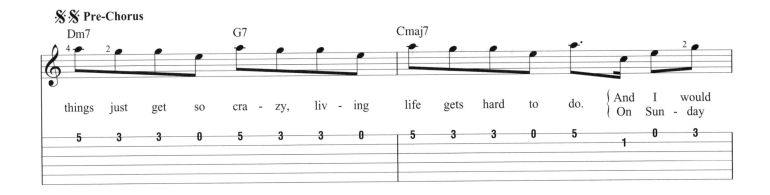

things just get so cra - zy, liv - ing life gets hard to do. { And I would / On Sun - day

glad - ly hit the road, get up and go if I knew that
morn - ing rain is fall - ing and I'm call - ing out to you, sing - ing,

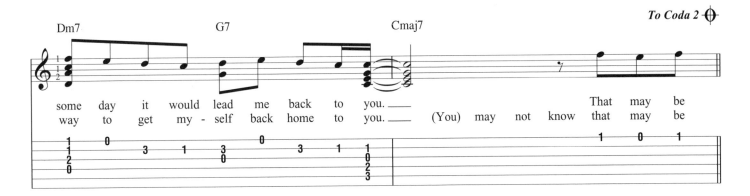

some day it would lead me back to you, ___ that
"Some day it will bring me back to you," ___ yeah. ___ Find a

To Coda 2

some day it would lead me back to you. ___ That may be
way to get my - self back home to you. ___ (You) may not know that may be

% Chorus

all I need. In dark - ness she is all I

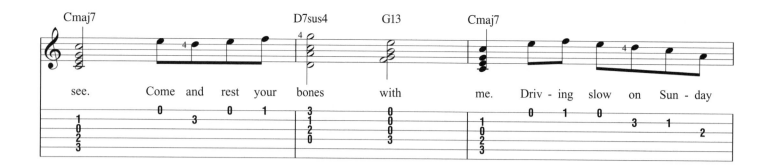

see. Come and rest your bones with me. Driv - ing slow on Sun - day

To Coda 1

Verse

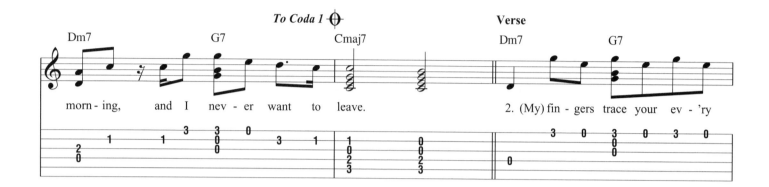

morn - ing, and I nev - er want to leave. 2. (My) fin - gers trace your ev - 'ry

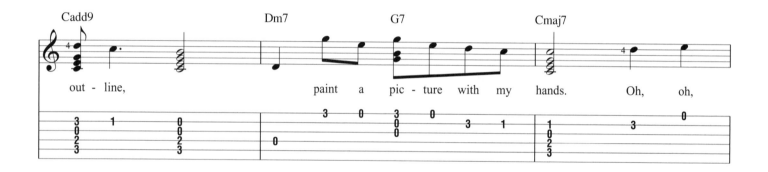

out - line, paint a pic - ture with my hands. Oh, oh,

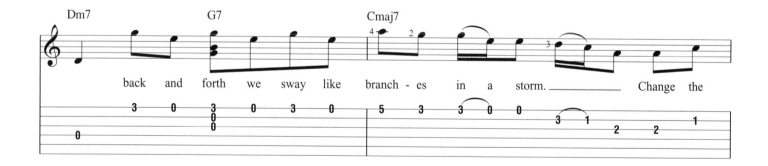

back and forth we sway like branch - es in a storm. _____ Change the

D.S. al Coda 1

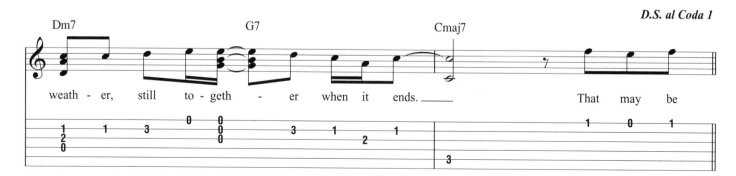

weath - er, still to - geth - er when it ends. _____ That may be

⊕ Coda 1

Interlude

⊕ Coda 2

D.S.S. al Coda 2

Outro-Chorus

w/ Lead Voc. ad lib. on repeats

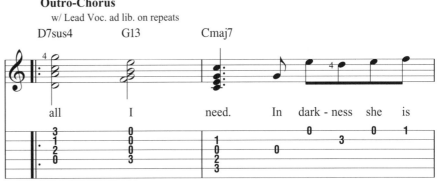

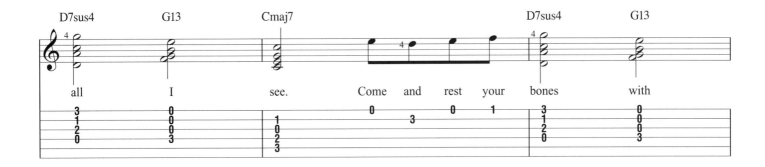

Repeat and fade

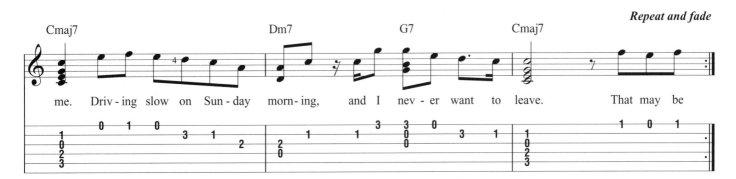

Wake Up Call

Words and Music by Adam Levine and James Valentine

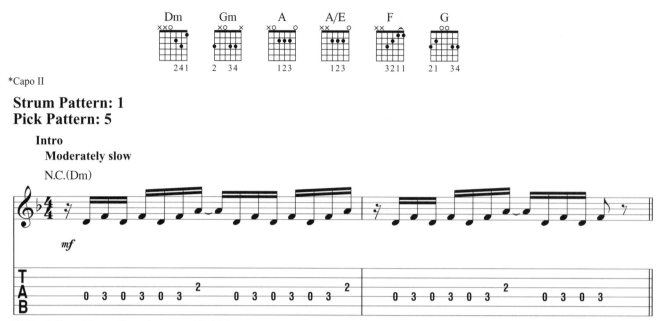

*Capo II

Strum Pattern: 1
Pick Pattern: 5

Intro
Moderately slow

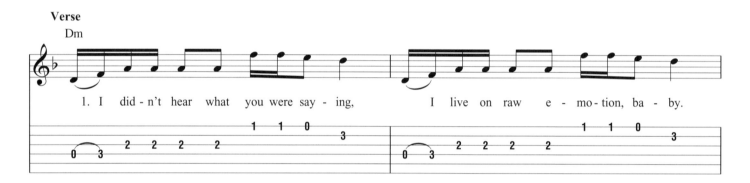

*Optional: To match recording, place capo at 2nd fret.

Verse

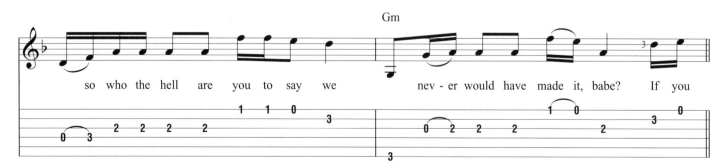

Pre-Chorus

need - ed love, well, then ask for love, could have giv - en love, now I'm tak - ing love. And it's

not my fault 'cause you both de - serve what is com - ing now, so don't say a word.

Chorus

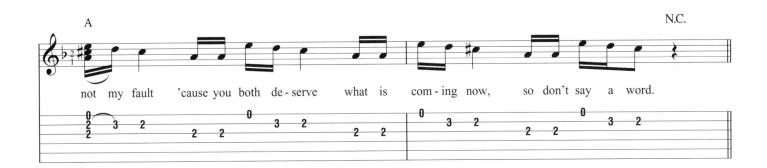

Wake up call, caught you in the morn - ing with an - oth - er one in my bed. Don't you

care a - bout me an - y - more, don't you care a - bout me? I don't think so.

Six foot tall, came with - out a warn - ing so I had to shoot him dead. He won't

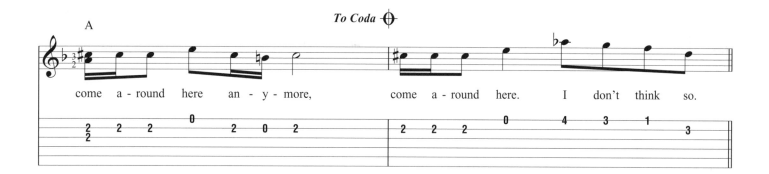

come a-round here an-y-more, come a-round here. I don't think so.

Verse

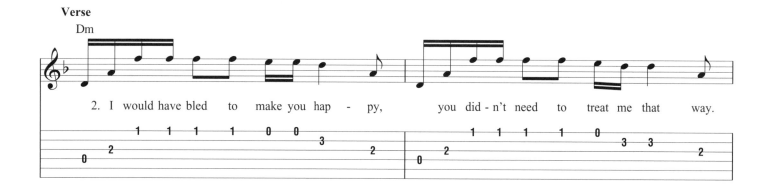

2. I would have bled to make you hap - py, you did-n't need to treat me that way.

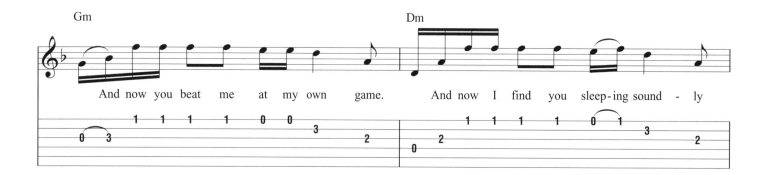

And now you beat me at my own game. And now I find you sleep-ing sound - ly

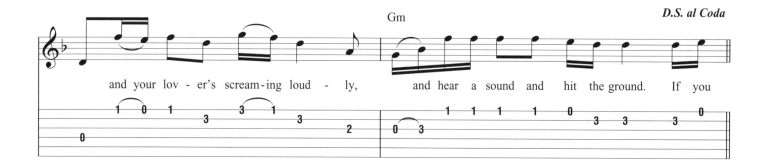

and your lov-er's scream-ing loud - ly, and hear a sound and hit the ground. If you

Coda

Bridge

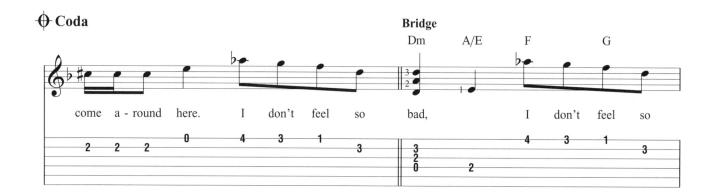

come a-round here. I don't feel so bad, I don't feel so

Won't Go Home Without You

Words and Music by Adam Levine

*Tune down 1/2 step:
(low to high) E♭-A♭-D♭-G♭-B♭-E♭

Strum Pattern: 1
Pick Pattern: 5

*Optional: To match recording, tune down 1/2 step.
**2nd time, substitute C#m7.

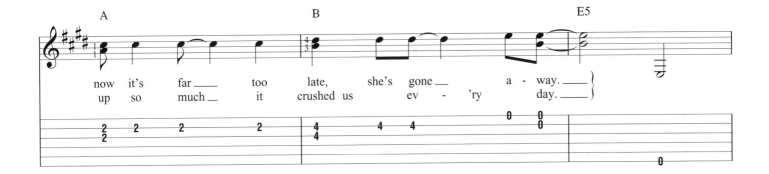

now it's far ____ too late, she's gone ____ a - way. ____
up so much ____ it crushed us ev - 'ry day. ____

Pre-Chorus

Ev - 'ry night ____ you cry your - self to sleep ____ think - ing why ____

____ does this hap - pen to me? ____ Why does ev - 'ry mo - ment

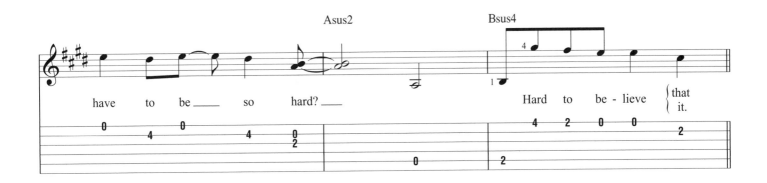

have to be ____ so hard? ____ Hard to be - lieve { that it.

% Chorus

it's } not o - ver to - night, ____ just give me one more chance to make ____ it right. ____
(3.) It's }

I may not make it through the night. __ I won't go home with-out __

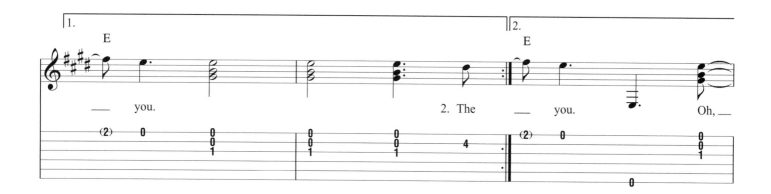

__ you.   2. The   __ you.   Oh, __

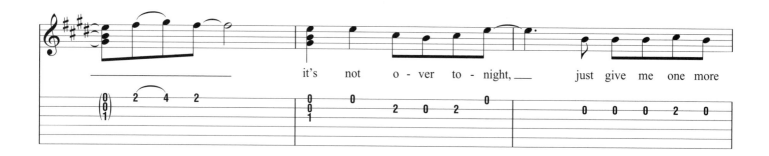

__   it's not o-ver to-night, __ just give me one more

chance to make __ it right. __   I may not make it through the night. __ I

To Coda ⊕

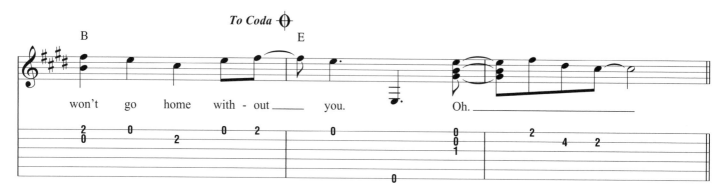

won't go home with-out __ you.   Oh. __

Bridge

And of all the things I've felt ___ but nev - er real - ly shown, ___

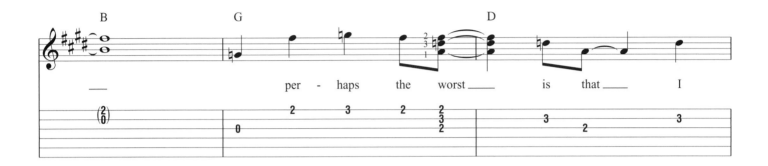

___ per - haps the worst ___ is that ___ I

D.S. al Coda
(take 2nd ending)

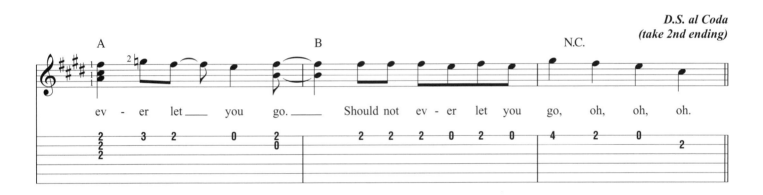

ev - er let ___ you go. ___ Should not ev - er let you go, oh, oh, oh.

⊕ Coda   **Outro**

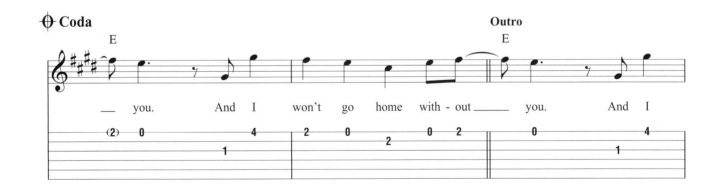

___ you.   And I won't go home with - out ___ you.   And I

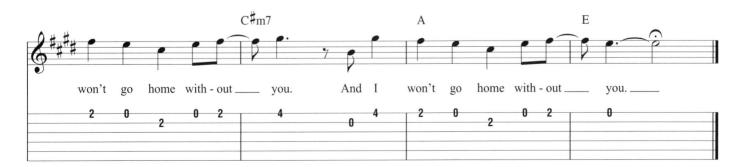

won't go home with - out ___ you.   And I won't go home with - out ___ you. ___

This Love

Words and Music by Adam Levine and Jesse Carmichael

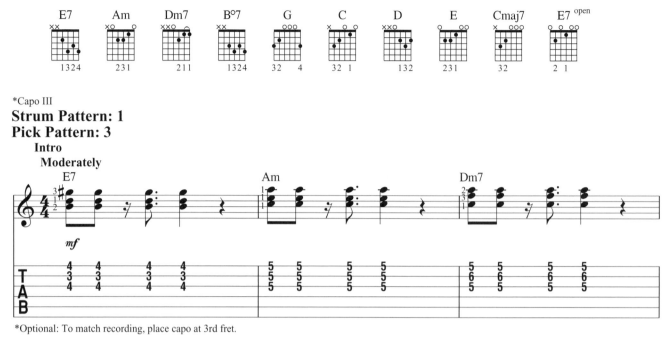

*Capo III

Strum Pattern: 1
Pick Pattern: 3

Intro
Moderately

*Optional: To match recording, place capo at 3rd fret.

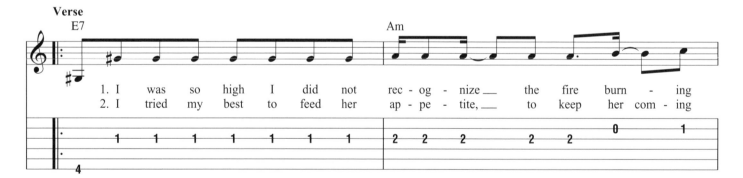

Verse

1. I was so high I did not rec-og-nize ___ the fire burn-ing
2. I tried my best to feed her ap-pe-tite, ___ to keep her com-ing

in her eyes. ___ The cha-os that con-trolled my mind.
ev-'ry night, ___ so hard to keep her sat-is-fied.

Whis-pered "Good-bye," as she got
Kept play-ing love like it was

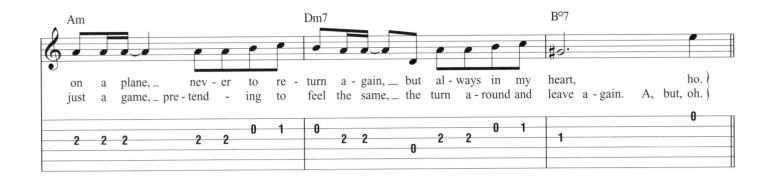

on a plane,＿ nev‑er to re‑turn a‑gain,＿ but al‑ways in my heart, ho.⎞

just a game,＿ pre‑tend – ing to feel the same,＿ the turn a‑round and leave a‑gain. A, but, oh.⎠

Chorus

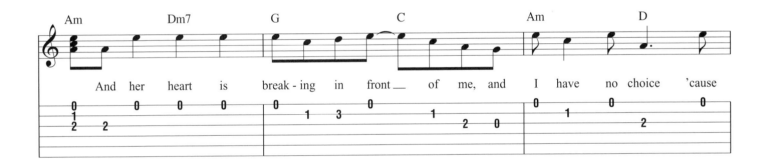

This love has tak‑en its toll＿ on me. She said, "Good‑bye," too man‑y times be‑fore.

And her heart is break‑ing in front＿ of me, and I have no choice 'cause

Interlude

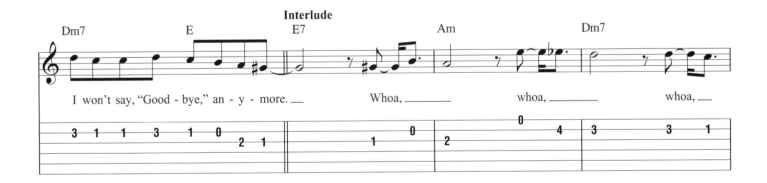

I won't say, "Good‑bye," an‑y‑more.＿ Whoa,＿ whoa,＿ whoa,

|1.| |2.| **Bridge**

whoa.＿ whoa.＿ I'll fix these bro‑ken things,

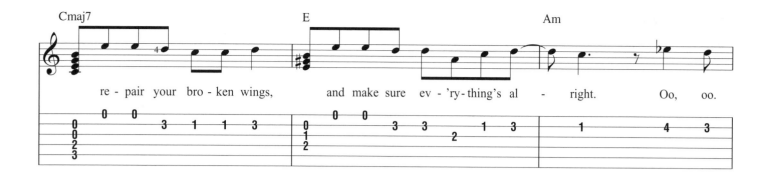

re - pair your bro - ken wings, and make sure ev - 'ry-thing's al - right. Oo, oo.

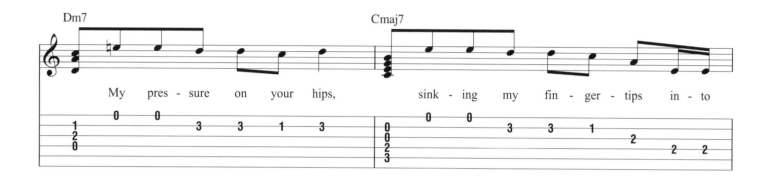

My pres - sure on your hips, sink - ing my fin - ger - tips in - to

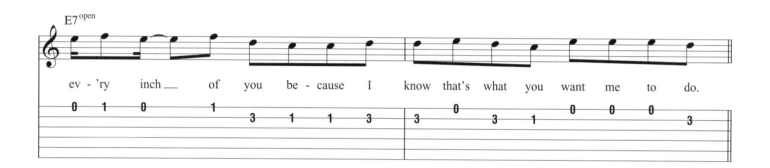

ev - 'ry inch __ of you be - cause I know that's what you want me to do.

Outro-Chorus

This love has tak - en its toll __ on me. She said, "Good - bye," too man - y times be - fore.

Repeat and fade

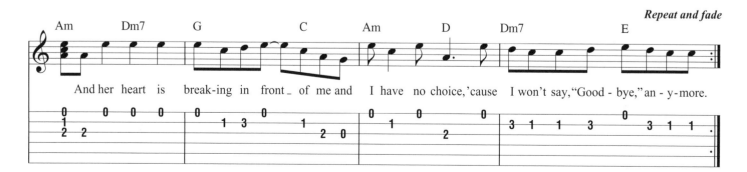

And her heart is break - ing in front __ of me and I have no choice, 'cause I won't say, "Good - bye," an - y - more.

EASY GUITAR WITH NOTES & TAB

This series features simplified arrangements with notes, tab, chord charts, and strum and pick patterns.

MIXED FOLIOS

00702287	Acoustic	$14.99
00702002	Acoustic Rock Hits for Easy Guitar	$12.95
00702166	All-Time Best Guitar Collection	$19.99
00699665	Beatles Best	$12.95
00702232	Best Acoustic Songs for Easy Guitar	$12.99
00119835	Best Children's Songs	$16.99
00702233	Best Hard Rock Songs	$14.99
00703055	The Big Book of Nursery Rhymes & Children's Songs	$14.99
00322179	The Big Easy Book of Classic Rock Guitar	$24.95
00698978	Big Christmas Collection	$16.95
00702394	Bluegrass Songs for Easy Guitar	$12.99
00703387	Celtic Classics	$14.99
00125023	Chart Hits of 2013-2014	$14.99
00118314	Chart Hits of 2012-2013	$14.99
00702149	Children's Christian Songbook	$7.95
00702237	Christian Acoustic Favorites	$12.95
00702028	Christmas Classics	$7.95
00101779	Christmas Guitar	$14.99
00702185	Christmas Hits	$9.95
00702141	Classic Rock	$8.95
00702203	CMT's 100 Greatest Country Songs	$27.95
00702283	The Contemporary Christian Collection	$16.99
00702006	Contemporary Christian Favorites	$9.95
00702239	Country Classics for Easy Guitar	$19.99
00702282	Country Hits of 2009–2010	$14.99
00702085	Disney Movie Hits	$12.95
00702257	Easy Acoustic Guitar Songs	$14.99
00702280	Easy Guitar Tab White Pages	$29.99
00702212	Essential Christmas	$9.95
00702041	Favorite Hymns for Easy Guitar	$9.95
00702281	4 Chord Rock	$9.99
00126894	Frozen	$14.99
00702286	Glee	$16.99
00699374	Gospel Favorites	$14.95
00122138	The Grammy Awards® Record of the Year 1958-2011	$19.99
00702160	The Great American Country Songbook	$15.99
00702050	Great Classical Themes for Easy Guitar	$6.95
00702116	Greatest Hymns for Guitar	$8.95
00702130	The Groovy Years	$9.95
00702184	Guitar Instrumentals	$9.95
00702273	Irish Songs	$12.99
00702275	Jazz Favorites for Easy Guitar	$14.99
00702274	Jazz Standards for Easy Guitar	$14.99
00702162	Jumbo Easy Guitar Songbook	$19.95
00702258	Legends of Rock	$14.99
00702261	Modern Worship Hits	$14.99
00702189	MTV's 100 Greatest Pop Songs	$24.95
00702272	1950s Rock	$14.99
00702271	1960s Rock	$14.99
00702270	1970s Rock	$14.99
00702269	1980s Rock	$14.99
00702268	1990s Rock	$14.99
00109725	Once	$14.99
00702187	Selections from O Brother Where Art Thou?	$12.95
00702178	100 Songs for Kids	$12.95
00702515	Pirates of the Caribbean	$12.99
00702125	Praise and Worship for Guitar	$9.95
00702155	Rock Hits for Guitar	$9.95
00702285	Southern Rock Hits	$12.99
00702866	Theme Music	$12.99
00121535	30 Easy Celtic Guitar Solos	$14.99
00702220	Today's Country Hits	$9.95
00702198	Today's Hits for Guitar	$9.95
00121900	Today's Women of Pop & Rock	$14.99
00702217	Top Christian Hits	$12.95
00103626	Top Hits of 2012	$14.99
00702294	Top Worship Hits	$14.99
00702206	Very Best of Rock	$9.95
00702255	VH1's 100 Greatest Hard Rock Songs	$27.99
00702175	VH1's 100 Greatest Songs of Rock and Roll	$24.95
00702253	Wicked	$12.99

ARTIST COLLECTIONS

00702267	AC/DC for Easy Guitar	$15.99
00702598	Adele for Easy Guitar	$14.99
00702001	Best of Aerosmith	$16.95
00702040	Best of the Allman Brothers	$14.99
00702865	J.S. Bach for Easy Guitar	$12.99
00702169	Best of The Beach Boys	$12.99
00702292	The Beatles — 1	$19.99
00125796	Best of Chuck Berry	$14.99
00702201	The Essential Black Sabbath	$12.95
02501615	Zac Brown Band — The Foundation	$16.99
02501621	Zac Brown Band — You Get What You Give	$16.99
00702043	Best of Johnny Cash	$16.99
00702291	Very Best of Coldplay	$12.99
00702263	Best of Casting Crowns	$12.99
00702090	Eric Clapton's Best	$10.95
00702086	Eric Clapton from the Album Unplugged	$10.95
00702202	The Essential Eric Clapton	$12.95
00702250	blink-182 — Greatest Hits	$12.99
00702053	Best of Patsy Cline	$10.95
00702229	The Very Best of Creedence Clearwater Revival	$14.99
00702145	Best of Jim Croce	$14.99
00702278	Crosby, Stills & Nash	$12.99
00702219	David Crowder*Band Collection	$12.95
14042809	Bob Dylan	$14.99
00702276	Fleetwood Mac — Easy Guitar Collection	$14.99
00130952	Foo Fighters	$14.99
00139462	The Very Best of Grateful Dead	$14.99
00702136	Best of Merle Haggard	$12.99
00702227	Jimi Hendrix — Smash Hits	$14.99
00702288	Best of Hillsong United	$12.99
00702236	Best of Antonio Carlos Jobim	$12.95
00702245	Elton John — Greatest Hits 1970–2002	$14.99
00129855	Jack Johnson	$14.99
00702204	Robert Johnson	$9.95
00702234	Selections from Toby Keith — 35 Biggest Hits	$12.95
00702003	Kiss	$9.95
00110578	Best of Kutless	$12.99
00702216	Lynyrd Skynyrd	$15.99
00702182	The Essential Bob Marley	$12.95
00702346	Bruno Mars — Doo-Wops & Hooligans	$12.99
00121925	Bruno Mars – Unorthodox Jukebox	$12.99
00702248	Paul McCartney — All the Best	$14.99
00702129	Songs of Sarah McLachlan	$12.95
00125484	The Best of MercyMe	$12.99
02501316	Metallica — Death Magnetic	$15.95
00702209	Steve Miller Band — Young Hearts (Greatest Hits)	$12.95
00124167	Jason Mraz	$14.99
00702096	Best of Nirvana	$14.99
00702211	The Offspring — Greatest Hits	$12.95
00138026	One Direction	$14.99
00702030	Best of Roy Orbison	$12.95
00702144	Best of Ozzy Osbourne	$14.99
00702279	Tom Petty	$12.99
00102911	Pink Floyd	$16.99
00702139	Elvis Country Favorites	$9.95
00702293	The Very Best of Prince	$12.99
00699415	Best of Queen for Guitar	$14.99
00109279	Best of R.E.M.	$14.99
00702208	Red Hot Chili Peppers — Greatest Hits	$12.95
00702093	Rolling Stones Collection	$17.95
00702196	Best of Bob Seger	$12.95
00702252	Frank Sinatra — Nothing But the Best	$12.99
00702010	Best of Rod Stewart	$14.95
00702049	Best of George Strait	$12.95
00702259	Taylor Swift for Easy Guitar	$14.99
00702260	Taylor Swift — Fearless	$12.99
00139727	Taylor Swift — 1989	$16.99
00115960	Taylor Swift — Red	$16.99
00702290	Taylor Swift — Speak Now	$15.99
00702262	Chris Tomlin Collection	$14.99
00702226	Chris Tomlin — See the Morning	$12.95
00702427	U2 — 18 Singles	$14.99
00102711	Van Halen	$16.99
00702108	Best of Stevie Ray Vaughan	$10.95
00702123	Best of Hank Williams	$12.99
00702111	Stevie Wonder — Guitar Collection	$9.95
00702228	Neil Young — Greatest Hits	$15.99
00119133	Neil Young — Harvest	$14.99
00702188	Essential ZZ Top	$10.95

Prices, contents and availability subject to change without notice.

7777 W. BLUEMOUND RD. P.O. BOX 13819 MILWAUKEE, WI 53213

Visit Hal Leonard online at
www.halleonard.com

0315

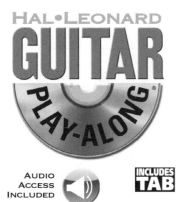

Hal·Leonard GUITAR PLAY-ALONG

AUDIO ACCESS INCLUDED

INCLUDES TAB

This series will help you play your favorite songs quickly and easily. Just follow the tab and listen to the CD or online audio to hear how the guitar should sound, and then play along using the separate backing tracks. Mac or PC users can also slow down the tempo without changing pitch by using the CD in their computer. The melody and lyrics are included in the book so that you can sing or simply follow along.

1. ROCK
00699570 Book/CD $16.99

2. ACOUSTIC
00699569 Book/CD $16.95

3. HARD ROCK
00699573 Book/CD $16.95

4. POP/ROCK
00699571 Book/CD $16.99

5. MODERN ROCK
00699574 Book/CD $16.99

6. '90s ROCK
00699572 Book/CD $16.99

7. BLUES
00699575 Book/CD $16.95

8. ROCK
00699585 Book/CD $14.99

10. ACOUSTIC
00699586 Book/CD $16.95

11. EARLY ROCK
0699579 Book/CD $14.95

12. POP/ROCK
00699587 Book/CD $14.95

13. FOLK ROCK
00699581 Book/CD $15.99

14. BLUES ROCK
00699582 Book/CD $16.95

15. R&B
00699583 Book/CD $14.95

16. JAZZ
00699584 Book/CD $15.95

17. COUNTRY
00699588 Book/CD $15.95

18. ACOUSTIC ROCK
00699577 Book/CD $15.95

19. SOUL
00699578 Book/CD $14.99

20. ROCKABILLY
00699580 Book/CD $14.95

21. YULETIDE
00699602 Book/CD $14.95

22. CHRISTMAS
00699600 Book/CD $15.95

23. SURF
00699635 Book/CD $14.95

24. ERIC CLAPTON
00699649 Book/CD $17.99

25. LENNON & McCARTNEY
00699642 Book/CD $16.99

26. ELVIS PRESLEY
00699643 Book/CD $14.95

27. DAVID LEE ROTH
00699645 Book/CD $16.95

28. GREG KOCH
00699646 Book/CD $14.95

29. BOB SEGER
00699647 Book/CD $15.99

30. KISS
00699644 Book/CD $16.99

31. CHRISTMAS HITS
00699652 Book/CD $14.95

32. THE OFFSPRING
00699653 Book/CD $14.95

33. ACOUSTIC CLASSICS
00699656 Book/CD $16.95

34. CLASSIC ROCK
00699658 Book/CD $16.95

35. HAIR METAL
00699660 Book/CD $16.95

36. SOUTHERN ROCK
00699661 Book/CD $16.95

37. ACOUSTIC METAL
00699662 Book/CD $22.99

38. BLUES
00699663 Book/CD $16.95

39. '80s METAL
00699664 Book/CD $16.99

40. INCUBUS
00699668 Book/CD $17.95

41. ERIC CLAPTON
00699669 Book/CD $16.95

42. 2000s ROCK
00699670 Book/CD $16.99

43. LYNYRD SKYNYRD
00699681 Book/CD $17.95

44. JAZZ
00699689 Book/CD $14.99

45. TV THEMES
00699718 Book/CD $14.95

46. MAINSTREAM ROCK
00699722 Book/CD $16.95

47. HENDRIX SMASH HITS
00699723 Book/CD $19.95

48. AEROSMITH CLASSICS
00699724 Book/CD $17.99

49. STEVIE RAY VAUGHAN
00699725 Book/CD $17.99

50. VAN HALEN 1978-1984
00110269 Book/CD $17.99

51. ALTERNATIVE '90s
00699727 Book/CD $14.99

52. FUNK
00699728 Book/CD $14.95

53. DISCO
00699729 Book/CD $14.99

54. HEAVY METAL
00699730 Book/CD $14.95

55. POP METAL
00699731 Book/CD $14.95

56. FOO FIGHTERS
00699749 Book/CD $15.99

57. SYSTEM OF A DOWN
00699751 Book/CD $14.95

58. BLINK-182
00699772 Book/CD $14.95

59. CHET ATKINS
00702347 Book/CD $16.99

60. 3 DOORS DOWN
00699774 Book/CD $14.95

61. SLIPKNOT
00699775 Book/CD $16.99

62. CHRISTMAS CAROLS
00699798 Book/CD $12.95

63. CREEDENCE CLEARWATER REVIVAL
00699802 Book/CD $16.99

64. OZZY OSBOURNE
00699803 Book/CD $16.99

66. THE ROLLING STONES
00699807 Book/CD $16.95

67. BLACK SABBATH
00699808 Book/CD $16.99

68. PINK FLOYD – DARK SIDE OF THE MOON
00699809 Book/CD $16.99

69. ACOUSTIC FAVORITES
00699810 Book/CD $14.95

70. OZZY OSBOURNE
00699805 Book/CD $16.99

71. CHRISTIAN ROCK
00699824 Book/CD $14.95

72. ACOUSTIC '90s
00699827 Book/CD $14.95

73. BLUESY ROCK
00699829 Book/CD $16.99

75. TOM PETTY
00699882 Book/CD $16.99

76. COUNTRY HITS
00699884 Book/CD $14.95

77. BLUEGRASS
00699910 Book/CD $14.99

78. NIRVANA
00700132 Book/CD $16.99

79. NEIL YOUNG
00700133 Book/CD $24.99

80. ACOUSTIC ANTHOLOGY
00700175 Book/CD $19.95

81. ROCK ANTHOLOGY
00700176 Book/CD $22.99

82. EASY ROCK SONGS
00700177 Book/CD $12.99

83. THREE CHORD SONGS
00700178 Book/CD $16.99

84. STEELY DAN
00700200 Book/CD $16.99

85. THE POLICE
00700269 Book/CD $16.99

86. BOSTON
00700465 Book/CD $16.99

87. ACOUSTIC WOMEN
00700763 Book/CD $14.99

88. GRUNGE
00700467 Book/CD $16.99

89. REGGAE
00700468 Book/CD $15.99

90. CLASSICAL POP
00700469 Book/CD $14.99

91. BLUES INSTRUMENTALS
00700505 Book/CD $14.99

92. EARLY ROCK INSTRUMENTALS
00700506 Book/CD $14.99

93. ROCK INSTRUMENTALS
00700507 Book/CD $16.99

94. SLOW BLUES
00700508 Book/CD $16.99

95. BLUES CLASSICS
00700509 Book/CD $14.99

96. THIRD DAY
00700560 Book/CD $14.95

97. ROCK BAND
00700703 Book/CD $14.99

98. ROCK BAND
00700704 Book/CD $14.95

99. ZZ TOP
00700762 Book/CD $16.99

100. B.B. KING
00700466 Book/CD $16.99

101. SONGS FOR BEGINNERS
00701917 Book/CD $14.99

102. CLASSIC PUNK
00700769 Book/CD $14.99

103. SWITCHFOOT
00700773 Book/CD $16.99

104. DUANE ALLMAN
00700846 Book/CD $16.99

106. WEEZER
00700958 Book/CD $14.99

107. CREAM
00701069 Book/CD $16.99

108. THE WHO
00701053 Book/CD $16.99

109. STEVE MILLER
00701054 Book/CD $14.99

110. SLIDE GUITAR HITS
00701055 Book/CD $16.99

111. JOHN MELLENCAMP
00701056 Book/CD $14.99

112. QUEEN
00701052 Book/CD $16.99

113. JIM CROCE
00701058 Book/CD $15.99

114. BON JOVI
00701060 Book/CD $14.99

115. JOHNNY CASH
00701070 Book/CD $16.99

116. THE VENTURES
00701124 Book/CD $14.99

117. BRAD PAISLEY
00701224 Book/CD $16.99

118. ERIC JOHNSON
00701353 Book/CD $16.99

119. AC/DC CLASSICS
00701356 Book/CD $17.99

120. PROGRESSIVE ROCK
00701457 Book/CD $14.99

121. U2
00701508 Book/CD $16.99

122. CROSBY, STILLS & NASH
00701610 Book/CD $16.99

123. LENNON & MCCARTNEY ACOUSTIC
00701614 Book/CD $16.99

124. MODERN WORSHIP
00701629 Book/CD $14.99

125. JEFF BECK
00701687 Book/CD $16.99

126. BOB MARLEY
00701701 Book/CD $16.99

127. 1970s ROCK
00701739 Book/CD $14.99

128. 1960s ROCK
00701740 Book/CD $14.99

129. MEGADETH
00701741 Book/CD $16.99

131. 1990s ROCK
00701743 Book/CD $14.99

132. COUNTRY ROCK
00701757 Book/CD $15.99

133. TAYLOR SWIFT
00701894 Book/CD $16.99

134. AVENGED SEVENFOLD
00701906 Book/CD $16.99

136. GUITAR THEMES
00701922 Book/CD $14.99

137. IRISH TUNES
00701966 Book/CD $15.99

138. BLUEGRASS CLASSICS
00701967 Book/CD $14.99

139. GARY MOORE
00702370 Book/CD $16.99

140. MORE STEVIE RAY VAUGHAN
00702396 Book/CD $17.99

141. ACOUSTIC HITS
00702401 Book/CD $16.99

144. DJANGO REINHARDT
00702531 Book/CD $16.99

145. DEF LEPPARD
00702532 Book/CD $16.99

147. SIMON & GARFUNKEL
14041591 Book/CD $16.99

148. BOB DYLAN
14041592 Book/CD $16.99

149. AC/DC HITS
14041593 Book/CD $17.99

150. ZAKK WYLDE
02501717 Book/CD $16.99

152. JOE BONAMASSA
02501751 Book/CD $19.99

153. RED HOT CHILI PEPPERS
00702990 Book/CD $19.99

155. ERIC CLAPTON – FROM THE ALBUM *UNPLUGGED*
00703085 Book/CD $16.99

156. SLAYER
00703770 Book/CD $17.99

157. FLEETWOOD MAC
00101382 Book/CD $16.99

158. ULTIMATE CHRISTMAS
00101889 Book/CD $14.99

160. T-BONE WALKER
00102641 Book/CD $16.99

161. THE EAGLES – ACOUSTIC
00102659 Book/CD $17.99

162. THE EAGLES HITS
00102667 Book/CD $17.99

163. PANTERA
00103036 Book/CD $16.99

166. MODERN BLUES
00700764 Book/CD $16.99

167. DREAM THEATER
00111938 Book/2-CD $24.99

168. KISS
00113421 Book/CD $16.99

169. TAYLOR SWIFT
00115982 Book/CD $16.99

170. THREE DAYS GRACE
00117337 Book/CD $16.99

171. JAMES BROWN
00117420 Book/CD $16.99

173. TRANS-SIBERIAN ORCHESTRA
00119907 Book/CD $19.99

174. SCORPIONS
00122119 Book/CD $16.99

176. BLUES BREAKERS WITH JOHN MAYALL & ERIC CLAPTON
00122132 Book/CD $19.99

177. ALBERT KING
00123271 Book/CD $16.99

178. JASON MRAZ
00124165 Book/CD $17.99

179. RAMONES
00127073 Book/CD $16.99

180. BRUNO MARS
00129706 Book/Audio $16.99

181. JACK JOHNSON
00129854 Book/CD $16.99

HAL•LEONARD® CORPORATION

7777 W. BLUEMOUND RD. P.O. BOX 13819 MILWAUKEE, WI 53213

For complete songlists, visit Hal Leonard online at
www.halleonard.com

Prices, contents, and availability subject to change without notice.

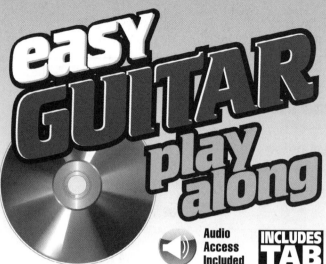

easy GUITAR play along

Audio Access Included

INCLUDES TAB

The **Easy Guitar Play Along®** Series features streamlined transcriptions of your favorite songs. Just follow the tab, listen to the audio to hear how the guitar should sound, and then play along using the backing tracks. The CD is playable on any CD player, and is also enhanced to include the Amazing Slowdowner technology so Mac and PC users can adjust the recording to any tempo without changing the pitch!

1. ROCK CLASSICS
Jailbreak • Living After Midnight • Mississippi Queen • Rocks Off • Runnin' Down a Dream • Smoke on the Water • Strutter • Up Around the Bend.
00702560 Book/CD Pack....... $14.99

2. ACOUSTIC TOP HITS
About a Girl • I'm Yours • The Lazy Song • The Scientist • 21 Guns • Upside Down • What I Got • Wonderwall.
00702569 Book/CD Pack....... $14.99

3. ROCK HITS
All the Small Things • Best of You • Brain Stew (The Godzilla Remix) • Californication • Island in the Sun • Plush • Smells like Teen Spirit • Use Somebody.
00702570 Book/CD Pack....... $14.99

4. ROCK 'N' ROLL
Blue Suede Shoes • I Get Around • I'm a Believer • Jailhouse Rock • Oh, Pretty Woman • Peggy Sue • Runaway • Wake up Little Susie.
00702572 Book/CD Pack..... $14.99

5. ULTIMATE ACOUSTIC
Against the Wind • Babe, I'm Gonna Leave You • Come Monday • Free Fallin' • Give a Little Bit • Have You Ever Seen the Rain? • New Kid in Town • We Can Work It Out.
00702573 Book/CD Pack........ $14.99

6. CHRISTMAS SONGS
Have Yourself a Merry Little Christmas • A Holly Jolly Christmas • The Little Drummer Boy • Run Rudolph Run • Santa Claus Is Comin' to Town • Silver and Gold • Sleigh Ride • Winter Wonderland.
00101879 Book/CD Pack......... $14.99

7. BLUES SONGS FOR BEGINNERS
Come On (Part 1) • Double Trouble • Gangster of Love • I'm Ready • Let Me Love You Baby • Mary Had a Little Lamb • San-Ho-Zay • T-Bone Shuffle.
00103235 Book/CD Pack..... $14.99

8. ACOUSTIC SONGS FOR BEGINNERS
Barely Breathing • Drive • Everlong • Good Riddance (Time of Your Life) • Hallelujah • Hey There Delilah • Lake of Fire • Photograph.
00103240 Book/CD Pack..... $14.99

9. ROCK SONGS FOR BEGINNERS
Are You Gonna Be My Girl • Buddy Holly • Everybody Hurts • In Bloom • Otherside • The Rock Show • Santa Monica • When I Come Around.
00103255 Book/CD Pack..... $14.99

10. GREEN DAY
Basket Case • Boulevard of Broken Dreams • Good Riddance (Time of Your Life) • Holiday • Longview • 21 Guns • Wake Me up When September Ends • When I Come Around.
00122322 Book/CD Pack..... $14.99

11. NIRVANA
All Apologies • Come As You Are • Heart Shaped Box • Lake of Fire • Lithium • The Man Who Sold the World • Rape Me • Smells like Teen Spirit.
00122325 Book/CD Pack..... $14.99

12. TAYLOR SWIFT
Fifteen • Love Story • Mean • Picture to Burn • Red • We Are Never Ever Getting Back Together • White Horse • You Belong with Me.
00122326 Book/CD Pack..... $16.99

14. JIMI HENDRIX – SMASH HITS
All Along the Watchtower • Can You See Me • Crosstown Traffic • Fire • Foxey Lady • Hey Joe • Manic Depression • Purple Haze • Red House • Remember • Stone Free • The Wind Cries Mary.
00130591 Book/Online Audio........ $24.99

HAL•LEONARD® CORPORATION
7777 W. BLUEMOUND RD. P.O. BOX 13819 MILWAUKEE, WI 53213

www.halleonard.com

Prices, contents, and availability subject to change without notice.